Published by
Bloomsbury USA, New York
Bloomsbury is a trademark of Bloomsbury Publishing Plc

All papers used by Bloomsbury USA are natural,
recyclable products made from wood grown in well-
managed forests. The manufacturing processes conform to
the environmental regulations of the country of origin.

Library of Congress Cataloging-in-Publication Data
has been applied for.

ISBN-13: 978-1-62040-256-6

First U.S. edition 2015

1 3 5 7 9 10 8 6 4 2

Designed and typeset by
Wooden Books Ltd, Glastonbury, UK

Printed in the U.S.A. by Worzalla,
Stevens Point, Wisconsin

LOVE

THE SONG OF THE UNIVERSE

Jason Martineau

BLOOMSBURY

NEW YORK · LONDON · NEW DELHI · SYDNEY

To lovers everywhere

All my love to Maryna Petrenko. Loving gratitude as ever to my parents and family. Special thanks to John Martineau and Stephen "Snips" Parsons for editing and layout. Thanks to Paul Taylor and Chiara Franceschini at the Warburg Institute in London. Though predominantly illustrated with male/female examples, the ideas in this book apply equally to same-sex relations.

Above: From The Rubáiyát of Omar Khayyam, *John Buckland Wright 1938.*
Title Page: Allegory of Venus, 1496. Venus exerts influence on some mortals drinking tea.
Frontispiece: Belle, Bonne, Sage, Chantilly Manuscript, Baude Cordier, 14th century.

CONTENTS

INTRODUCTION

What is love? Why do we experience it? We love friends, parents, movies, songs, ideas, pets, nature, work, and of course lovers…the list is endless, but can it be understood in any meaningful terms?

The ancient Greeks pondered this and came up with a variety of definitions: *Eros*, which is sexual love; *Philia*, a mutual love between friends and family; *Agape*, a selfless love for everyone or God; and *Storge*, a natural affection which can be applied equally to the non-human world. Other variations include: *Epithumia* (lust), *Ludus* (playful love), *Pragma* (long-standing love), and *Philautia* (love of the self).

Students of mythology, biology, sociobiology, and psychology regularly explore the subject from a multitude of perspectives, so the basic tenets of love, its effects and place in society, are well-documented, although its essence remains enigmatic.

Love is variously cultivated, received, given, and experienced through body, heart, and mind, causing rapture, radiance, or even illness and madness. Love can be pious, committed, dutiful, demanding, tender, remote, faded, ecstatic, invigorating, exhausting, and so much more. Love asks that we open ourselves to its beautiful and profound mystery, and at the same time to its potential loss.

Love is not to be taken lightly. The Greek god of love, Eros, famously shot Apollo with a golden arrow in revenge for being mocked by him, causing an endless unrequited yearning for the nymph Daphne (who took the form of a laurel tree to evade her unwanted suitor). The evergreen laurel remains a symbol of chastity, poetry, and music. Mortals take care! The song of the universe sings to us all…

MOTHER AND FATHER

who made you

Our first love is for our mother. She gives us life, holds us, and we gaze into her eyes when she feeds us. As infants, our dependence upon her is greatest and she instills our sense of safety. Through her we learn to trust and be trusted (*see page 36*).

Horticultural and agricultural societies throughout early history worship the Great Mother goddess, the provisioning and nurturing aspect of nature. In Egyptian, Babylonian, and Hindu cosmology, as well as in Greek and Roman mythology and other traditions, the role of the divine feminine is of great significance. In Christianity, Judaism, and Islam, she becomes Mary, Miriam, and Maryam respectively - mother of Jesus. She can also be fearsome and destructive: the Hindu goddess Kali wears a necklace of severed heads and represents both life and death (*see opposite*). Likewise, the Egyptian goddess Isis is considered a sublime mother and protector of the dead.

The next person we meet is Father. The psychologist Erich Fromm [1900-1980] stated that through him we learn conditionality, rules, and how to relate to the world. Mythological fathers like Zeus, Jove, Jehovah, Yahweh, and the Roman god Saturn can be judgmental, punishing, loving, or benevolent. Freud [1856-1939] believed that all children go through a phase of fixating on their opposite sex parent, while Jung [1875-1961] suggested that these personalities help to form core parts of our internal psyche: the *anima* (female) and *animus* (male).

With one complete set of 23 chromosomes from each parent in every cell of their bodies, few people can deny the profound formative importance of mother and father.

*Isis with her son Horus.
Compare with below.*

*Mother and Child.
Japan 1739.*

*Kali. The sword (wisdom)
slices the head (ego).*

*Above: Mary with child. Note the crescent
moon, symbol of the divine feminine.*

*Above: God the father and creator, by Giulio
Bonasone, Bologna, 1574.*

FAMILY
siblings and grandparents

After parents, the closest people for many are brothers and sisters. For those lucky enough to have any, these chicks from the same nest can either become the very closest of friends, or the source of endless difficulties and complex emotions.

The idea of "brotherhood" is widely evoked by various institutions and religions. Brotherly love can extend beyond immediate family to "blood brothers", close friends who touch bleeding thumbs to share blood. The "sisterhood" is similarly universal, and sisterly love between female friends can be just as powerful as the love between biological sisters, and less competitive.

Philial love (*see page 1*) also includes grandparents, often a rich source of wisdom, humor, and stories. The love between grandparents and grandchildren can be especially uncomplicated and treasured. A strong sense of kin creates security and reinforces traits and habits.

Conditioning (via reward and punishment) and *imprinting* (attaching and copying) occur in youngsters across the animal world. Love, as expressed by family members, is therefore of profound significance.

Above: Childhood games can resurface in adult life. Codex Manesse, c. 1304-40.

Above: Hugging releases vasopressin and oxytocin and is learned early.

Above: The British royal family, 1877. Kinship strengthens the sense of belonging, while intergenerational exchanges enrich all ages.

HOME SWEET HOME
east, west, home is best

The smell of home cooking, the warm embrace of parents, the sound of the old clock ticking, the sight of Mother's face, the feeling of clean sheets, the sound of a nearby stream or the blanket of a starry night. As Dorothy says in *The Wizard of Oz*, "There's no place like home." But what actually is a home?

Warmth, familiarity, and safety all contribute to a strong foundation in which love can grow, but these are not solely connected with a permanent abode or family base. A myriad of locations - or even people - can "feel like home," and passions surrounding ideas of homeland, home country, or home planet deepen the concept further. Just as missing your beloved (*see page 30*) can have strong physiological effects, being away from this essential place of refuge can also be painful; homesickness proves that home is where the heart is.

In a similar way the idea of "home truths" hints that every life story is set somewhere. Homes are where these stories happen and where memories are anchored, even those of leaving an old home to find and create a new one. If lucky, a good home, filled with love, will also play host to life's final scene.

John Bowlby [1907-1990] suggested that people develop one of four basic attachment patterns which inform their adult lives and loves: *Proximity Maintenance* (the desire to be near the one attached to); *Safe Haven* (returning to the attachment figure for comfort and safety in the face of a fear or threat); *Secure Base* (the attachment figure is a reliable home from which the world can be explored); and *Separation Distress* (anxiety is felt when the attachment figure is absent).

Above: The excitement of Daddy coming home. Dalziels, 1862. Mommy's turn tomorrow.

Above: Telemachus embraces his father Odysseus. P. Wilson, 1911.

Above: Home comforts. J. Tissot, 1882. Participating in regular expressions of affection is good for everyone.

Above: Home is where the heart is. Two lovers c. 1630, Iran.

BIOPHILIA
it's in our nature

In all countries and climates, people find themselves attracted to the nourishing quality of natural life, whether it be mountain streams, woodlands of flowers, fresh fruits, the surf on a beach, or the simple act of keeping plants and flowers in or around the home.

People seek deep affiliations with other living systems, rooted, according to biologist Edward O. Wilson [b. 1929], in human biology. "Love of nature" (*biophilia*) is part of our genetic makeup, and natural environments enable humanity to survive and thrive. Yet at the same time, nature is red in tooth and claw; life consumes and destroys life in order to sustain and create more life. A love for nature therefore can enrich and inform a person's love for life itself.

As a counterpoint to materialism, artists, poets, writers, and musicians often express a Romantic desire to "return to the forgotten sources of life." Henry David Thoreau [1817-1862] writes "Heaven is under our feet as well as over our heads."

Above: Oriental landscape, Japan, c.1502. *Opposite:* A youth asleep, surrounded by nature, 1766.

Above: The Little Garden of Love, c.1450. *Courtship surrounded by nature doing the same.*

THE EXTENDED TRIBE
loving animals

Did you have a dog when you were growing up? Or a cat? Or a bird, snake, or tarantula? Can you remember how you felt when they died? In fairy tales, people who are kind to animals do fine, while others who are cruel to our furry, feathered, or scaly friends fare less well.

In humans, emotions are experienced with the help of the *limbic system*, where sensory impressions are processed by the *hippocampus* and the *amygdala*, and interpreted as either painful or pleasurable, safe or dangerous, before forming into long-term memories in the cognitive *neocortex*. These help us to learn about the world, to socialize, and to survive. All mammals have some form of limbic system (*in the orca, below, it is more developed than in humans*), so complex emotional and group behavior in the animal world is widely observed, and bonds between humans and animals, whether for survival or companionship, are commonplace. Wolves, for example, allied with humans to later become household friends.

Above: "My sisters, the birds" - Saint Francis of Assisi is perhaps the most famous exponent of communication with animals. People sometimes love their pets with greater intensity than their more loquacious biological counterparts.

Below: Feline charms and voluptuous languor in La Paresse (laziness) by Felix Vallotton, 1896.

Above: Fragonard's 1775 drawing Oh! If Only He Were as Faithful to Me. Artists from this era often depict a dog to reinforce the image of a jilted human subject.

Below: Jilted by Briton Riviere, 1887. Another case of canine solace. In times of intense emotional stress animals can be of great comfort.

FRIENDS
are forever

The ancient Greeks placed the idea of friendship within *philial* love (*see page 1*), defining a spectrum of mutual regard from utility (as in business), to pleasure (shared activities), up to deep camaraderie (loyalty and sacrifice), and beyond. Aristotle describes friendship as wanting what is good for your friends and helping them to get it.

In the Sufi poetry of Rumi and Hafiz "friend" is used interchangeably with "beloved," indicating a relationship with God. Similarly Thomas Aquinas states that the Christian habit of *caritas* (charity) extends "not only to the love of God, but also to the love of our neighbor."

Friends may wish to be careful of romance. In the story of *Pyramus and Thisbe* from Ovid's *Metamorphoses*, two childhood friends and neighbors fall in love as they reach young adulthood. However, their families forbid them to be together. In the scene opposite (*lower left*), Thisbe discovers Pyramus, who has killed himself in despair after seeing a lion with her veil in its bloody jaws (she had dropped it there earlier while drinking from a stream). Upon finding him there lifeless, Thisbe takes her own life. This story inspired Shakespeare's *Romeo and Juliet*.

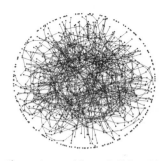

Above: A typical "extended" friendship network from Alam & Meyer, 2006. Research by Robin Dunbar suggests most people can't have more than 150 close friends.

Above: Friendship is Equality, c.1520. A friend is another self, loving and true.

Left: Pyramus and Thisbe, friends who fall in love, by Hans Schäufelein, 1480-1540.

Below: School scene, Amsterdam, 17th century.

Chemical Reactions
you're cute

Remember your first crush? Teenagers, arrested by physical attraction, experience an earth-shattering cascade of chemicals rushing through their brains, minds, and bodies. They can't sleep, their emotions fluctuate wildly, and they find communication with adults difficult. Their skin excretes pheromones, scents which communicate health information to those around them. Scientific studies have repeatedly shown that women are most attracted to the smell of men who have immune systems exhibiting the greatest variations from their own. The urge to procreate is driven, at the chemical level, by hormones – *testosterone* for men, and *estrogen* and *progesterone* for women.

Touching and emotional intimacy stimulate the production of the neurohormones *vasopressin* and *oxytocin*, both increasing feelings of bonding and trust. The neurotransmitters *dopamine*, *norepinephrine*, and *serotonin* bind to receptors in the brain bringing pleasure and increasing motivation, while *adrenaline* gets us giddy.

The beautiful pastoral love story of *Daphnis and Chloe* (*opposite*), written by Longus in Greece around 200 AD, appears to typify the heady mix of chemical reaction and subliminal connection which is felt so strongly in the early stages of love.

Above: Daphnis and Chloe grow up together, fall in love, yet are unaware of what is happening. They are told that the only cure for this strange feeling is to kiss. After many trials and tribulations, they eventually marry. Laugier, 1817.

ALWAYS ON MY MIND
love looks not only with the eyes

While neurochemistry powerfully affects our *brains*, words, thoughts, and ideas make lasting impressions upon our *minds*.

In the infamous real-life story of *Heloise and Abelard* from 12th-century France, Abelard, a gifted philosopher, finds himself falling for his erudite student Heloise, who is likewise enthralled by him (*see opposite top left*). They fall deeply in love. Heloise becomes pregnant and they secretly marry, but the scandal is later discovered and Abelard is eventually castrated by Heloise's family (although Abelard claimed that the pain of parting was the greater). Separated, the pair continue their love by writing profoundly beautiful letters, a testament to the deep love between their two souls.

The American psychologist Dorothy Tennov [1928-2007] created the word "limerence" to describe how our thoughts and feelings can at times be overwhelming and uncontrollable when falling in love. Reciprocation by the limerent object (the other person) is of the utmost importance. This mutual fascination helps to kickstart love and push the two individuals closer together.

The classic 1756 version of *Beauty and the Beast*, by Madame LePrince de Beaumont, describes how seeing beyond physical appearance can open the door to love. Belle, pure of heart, at first only sees the ugly Beast as a friend, despite his kind personality and fervent wish to marry her. Leaving him for her sick father, she returns to find him dying from a broken heart. She suddenly realizes her love for him and kisses him, effecting his transformation into the handsome prince he has really been all along (*see opposite lower left*).

Left: Heloise and Abelard's beautiful minds bonding; their love survives physical decoupling. Right: Prince Jürgen and a deeply pensive tree nymph. J.B. Wright, 1949.

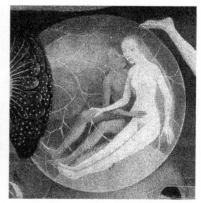

Above: It's what's inside that counts. Beast restored by beauty's kiss. 1908.

Above: Lovers in their bubble. Hieronymous Bosch, c. 1500.

IT TAKES TWO TO TANGO

shall we dance?

Courtship rituals are prominent throughout the animal world (*e.g. see peacock, opposite lower right*) and humans are no exception. Whether at a nightclub or wedding, dancing holds special importance in the annals of love. Close body synchrony allows two partners to show off their intellectual and physical vitality via the symmetry and balance of their movements. Rhythmically moving together also attunes dancers to each other and cultivates shared intentions. Research by contemporary neurobiologist Dr. Aniruddh Patel suggests that the only creatures that can move to a beat are ones that can mimic sounds: some birds, dolphins, whales, and people.

The *Rasa Lili* divine love dance of Classical Hindu scripture describes how young Gopi females, upon hearing Krishna playing his flute in the forest, leave their homes to dance for a night lasting billions of years. Romantic love is seen as a reflection of this eternal, spiritual love.

Most ancient dances are group dances, promoting cooperation and group consciousness. The Etruscan dancers below are from a tomb painting in the Grotta del Triclinio [c. 600 BC].

Above: Village dancers, 1609, France. When it comes to finding a partner, few activities offer more opportunities than dancing!

Above: Tarantella in Southern Italy. Part of this ancient dance involves the male acting out an entrancing courtship as he moves around the dominant female.

Below: A male peacock attempts to catch the eye of a peahen. Maruyama Okyo, Japan, 1781.

Below: Learning the moves. A couple learning to dance together. An enjoyable way to deepen the acquaintance.

WHY PEOPLE MEET
déjà vu, destiny, and karma

Often when people fall in love they describe a sense of familiarity about the other person, as though they are a long-lost friend. Some couples believe that forces of astrology, predestination, or the *karma* of past lives brought them together (similar to *metempsychosis*, the ancient Greek notion of the transmigration of souls). Thus two people who may have caused harm to one another in a previous life may fall in love in the present life to heal the ancient wounds (or create new ones!). Such *karma* is said to operate with the assistance of the wheel of psychological archetypes, the subject of astrology, with souls reincarnating at the precise time and place required for the job at hand. Coincidence, luck, and serendipity can all merge into such explanations.

Another explanation involves *transference*, where feelings or memories about someone from the past (often a parent or childhood friend) are triggered by, and then redirected toward, the new object of desire. Transference can aid attraction and bonding, and afford an opportunity to reclaim something lost, or heal something injured.

In the Chinese legend of *The Butterfly Lovers* two young children, Zhu Tingtai and Liang Shanbo, meet at school. Since girls, at this time, are not allowed to be educated, Zhu disguises herself as a boy. She falls in love with Liang, while Liang regards Zhu, her true identity hidden, like a brother. It takes many months before Zhu reveals the truth, and the two then swear undying love.

The theme of star-crossed lovers is common in ancient literature. Overcoming one's stars can require a strong will. All too often, as Shakespeare writes, "the fault... is not in our stars, but in ourselves."

Above: The Young White King and His Queen Learning Each Other's Language, 1516. *Language exchanges remain popular to this day.*

Above: The Three Norns of Norse mythology *are said to rule over what is, what was, and what should be. Ludwig Berger, 1882.*

Above: Not meant to be, The Butterfly Lovers. *Despite undying love, the union is forbidden. Zhu is married off and Liang dies heartbroken.*

Above: A love destined to embrace ecstasy and tragedy. Troilus kisses his beloved Criseyde. William Morris, 1896.

THE FOOD OF LOVE
seductive modes and melodies

The troubadours, trouveres, meistersingers, and minnesingers of the high medieval era were traveling poets and musicians who performed their works for the noble classes. The songs dealt with topics such as veiled seduction, ribaldry, illicit or unrequited love, and chivalry. At times they sublimated love itself into a form of sacred art. The ideals they shaped are the foundation of Western poetry and love songs.

One heartbreaking tale from Greek legend features Orpheus – the father of songs – who had the ability to charm all living things (even stones) with his music. His attempt to retrieve his dead true love Eurydice from the underworld ends in tragedy, despite softening the hearts of Hades and Persephone with his beautiful melodies.

The Sirens (*see below*) of Greek mythology would lure nearby sailors to shipwreck with their enchanting music and voices. The Greeks, like many cultures of antiquity, believed strongly in the power of music.

The famous wedding processional known as "Here Comes the Bride" is the "Bridal Chorus" from Wagner's 1850 opera *Lohengrin*. Less well-known is the fact that in the story it is followed by the murder of several guests at the wedding!

Above: Musicians from a 13th-century French manuscript psalter.

Above: Greek Muses. Calliope (poetry) and Euterpe (music). Note they both play the flute.

Above: Priapus conducting, from Hypnerotomachia Poliphili, F. Colonna, 1499.

Right: Orpheus plays his lyre to Eurydice. Orpheus is the son of Apollo, the Greek god of music.

EXCHANGING GIFTS
giving, receiving, and returning

The exchanging of gifts can be a profound and pleasurable feature of courtship. In Neoplatonic theory, the Three Graces (*opposite top left*) embody the threefold aspect of generosity: the giving, receiving, and returning of gifts or benefits. In one of his *Essays*, Seneca [4 BC - AD 65] remarks of the *gratia,* "Why do the sisters hand in hand dance in a ring which returns upon itself? For the reason that a benefit passing in its course from hand to hand returns nevertheless to the giver."

St. Valentine's Day owes its existence to the 3rd-century Roman saint Valentinus, who was jailed for officiating secret wedding ceremonies for soldiers forbidden to marry; he was executed on February 14th. The next day was the pagan fertility holiday Lupercalia, in honor of the god Lupercus (the Roman equivalent of the Greek god Pan). A lottery was held on this day during which young women's names were written on little slips of paper, then drawn randomly by young men to select who would be their companions for the rest of the year. This practice often led to marriage. The combination of these two auspicious days eventually evolved into the giving of paper cards or valentines. The *Scherenshnitte* (scissor cut) valentine originated in Germany and Switzerland in the 16th century (*see opposite top right*).

A suitor may also choose to say it with flowers. Popular across Europe in the 18th and 19th centuries, floriography, "the language of flowers," uses different blooms and floral arrangements to send coded love messages. Purple lilac, for example, symbolized "*first emotions of love*." The word "flirt" derives from the French "fleurette," the bouquet that aspiring troubadours gave to the objects of their passions.

Left: The Three Graces also represent soul, body, and spirit. Marco Da Ravenna, 1515.

Right: Scherenshnitte paper-cutting, c. 1600, Germany.

Below: The Garden of Love, medieval woodcut. The woman on the right appears to be reading a love note.

TESTS AND TRIALS
the course of true love never runs smoothly

Trials, obstacles, and dramas often appear in the early stages of love, a pattern which is reflected in stories across the world. In a definitive example, Psyche (Greek goddess of the soul) is given a series of tests by Venus to prove herself worthy of Cupid's hand in marriage. In one instance Psyche has to sort a large mound of different seeds in one night, a task she manages with the assistance of ants. With occasional help from nature she completes all the tests, and Venus approves the union. The metaphor is clear - when the soul is pure in its commitment to love, everything aligns to ensure its success. Heroic struggle also features strongly in the literature of medieval courtly love.

In the Russian fairy tale *The Maiden Tsar*, Ivan sets out to find his true love, who has already promised to marry him, but has since sailed far away. To find her, he undergoes a series of tests, each more challenging than the previous. He is then advised to find a firebird (symbolizing transformation and rebirth), which carries him to the sea. Eventually he finds his maiden's love (and her trust), hidden in an egg, in a duck, in a hare, in a box, in an oak tree!

The import of all such challenges is partly allegorical: lovers must overcome the obstacles created by the resistance of their own egos. In another tale from the East, *Snegurochka*, the Snow Maiden falls in love with the boy flute player Lel, but has to melt her frozen heart and "die" in order to be able to feel her love.

Tests and trials can also be frustratingly mundane: disapproving in-laws, jealous suitors, physical and cultural divides, or financial hurdles. If your love is true, be resolute, or you may forever wonder "what if?"

Above: Odysseus has to undertake an epic journey to return home to his beloved Penelope, and when he finally gets there she is surrounded by suitors whom he must slay. J. Flaxman, 1805.

Above: French carving c. 1340, showing a maiden defending her honor with flowers. Heroic deeds, valor, death, lust, and virtuous rejection are prominent themes in courtly love.

THE KISS
transformation

"How delicious is the winning of a kiss at Love's beginning," writes the poet Thomas Campbell. Kissing is an expression of approval. Kissing a fruit offered to a stranger proves its edibility, and kissing a hand, cheek, foot, or tongue allows the parties to assess each other's scent and taste. Saliva contains over one thousand proteins containing markers of physical health and genetic makeup.

The lips have more nerves for their area than any other part of the body, followed by the tongue and fingers. The supersensitive top border of the upper lip is sometimes called "cupid's bow," and kissing on the lips for any extended period of time is widely considered a first step towards sexual intimacy.

In the popular tale of *The Frog Prince*, a princess drops her golden ball into a pond. She offers a frog anything in the kingdom if he will retrieve it. He asks for a kiss, and she agrees, but later goes back on her word. After he hops up to the palace, her father reminds her to keep her word, so she kisses the frog and he transforms into a prince.

Above: Kiss, by Eric Gill, 1927.

Above: It's not only frogs that transform. In The She-bear by Giambattista Basile (1634), a widowed king chooses to remarry his own daughter, the only woman as beautiful as her mother. To escape, the terrified girl eats a magic chip of wood which changes her into a bear. Later, a Prince finds her in the woods. They kiss, she is restored, and they ultimately marry.

Above: Public kissing. A couple daring to demonstrate affection. The Lovers, c. 1450.

WHEN LOVERS PART
from a pair to two halves

Separation from one's beloved is never easy. The story of *Layla and Majnun*, by the 12th-century Persian poet Nazami, is a quintessential tale of forbidden love where absence and intense yearning acquire a spiritual dimension. Qays and Layla encounter each other as children, grow up together, fall in love, but are told by Layla's father that marriage will not be permitted. Tormented by this decree, and with his his heart breaking, Qays runs into the wild and lives among the animals, all of whom gradually become his companions and followers. He loses weight, and starts to go mad (thus his nickname Majnun, madman). Majnun wanders the desert, chanting poems about Layla, which people come from wide and far to hear. Layla eventually hears these poems, and writes cryptic answers to him on fragments of paper, praying that the wind will carry them to him. Majnun's father takes him to Mecca, hoping to wake him from this endless torment, but Majnun instead prays that his love for Layla should intensify, transforming it into a profoundly spiritual love.

Philosophy, both ancient and modern, speculates that the underlying current of romantic love is a yearning for a sense of completion. Dr. Aaron Ben Zeév identifies three features of incompleteness: wanting the relationship upgraded (or resumed); believing that it is lacking something; and believing that completeness is possible if both parties strive to become "whole." In comparing courtly love, cyber love, and extramarital affairs, he found that in each case an element is missing — consummation, physical proximity, or future viability (respectively) — all of which can lead to increased emotional intensity.

Above: An unknown woman yearns for her lover, 1865. Absence makes the heart grow fonder.

Above: A dramatic parting, 1783. Never easy tearing yourself away.

Left: Layla sits with Majnun in the wild, 14th c. Right: Layla pines, 18th C. Without her beloved to help stimulate the production of oxytocin, dopamine, and serotonin, she feels terrible.

SYNCHRONICITY
essential empathy

When in love, some people become more sensitized to other people's emotional states (while others become less so). The personal intimacy enjoyed by lovers can give them a fresh perspective on the world. Empathy is assisted by specialized cortical nerve cells, *mirror neurons*, which help with the processing of other peoples' feelings and intentions (e.g. the apparent involuntary contagion of smiles and yawns, or the ability to sense when someone is looking at you from afar).

In Dante's *Divine Comedy*, Francesca is married to Paolo's unpleasant brother Gianciotto. One day Francesca and Paolo are in a field reading a book about Lancelot and Guinevere, when they discover they are deeply in love. Their subsequent adultery is discovered, and both are killed by Gianciotto. Destined to be together in the second ring of hell (Lust) for all eternity, Dante asks of them how something so beautiful and pure as love could bring this fate. Francesca replies, "There is no greater pain than to remember, in our present grief, past happiness."

Long-time lovers often come to resemble each other over time (*opposite top right*). This is sometimes explained via shared lifestyle factors such as diet and exercise, or behavioral mimicry, where positive reinforcement patterns, such as laughing and smiling together, cause special lines around the face (*Duchenne* smiles) to form. Again we see the action of mirror neurons and empathy, both vital to love.

Left: Paolo and Francesca da Rimini, from Dante's Divine Comedy.

Right: Tenderly tuning in, The Ninth Month, *Boilly, 1807*

Below: Love is in the air in this delightful Court d'Amour, Orsini, *16th C. Italy.*

COMPLETELY IN LOVE
or not even slightly

_____

Love changes everything. "Love is an irresistible desire to be irresistibly desired," wrote Robert Frost; "Life without love is like a tree without blossoms or fruit," said Khalil Gibran, while Lao Tzu stated that "Being loved by someone deeply gives you strength, while loving someone deeply gives you courage." The type of love you may be currently experiencing can be assessed using the diagram opposite.

In the 16th-century story of *Salim and Anarkali*, Prince Salim falls in love with the beautiful dancing girl Anarkali, but Salim's father, Akbar the Great, prohibits their marriage and tries to discredit her. In response Salim declares war against his father, and loses. Rather than hand over Anarkali, he chooses execution, but at the last moment she renounces their love and sacrifices her own life so that Salim will live.

When it comes to love at first sight, few can rival Dante. If his own account is to be believed, he meets his beloved Beatrice only twice; first when they are children, then briefly in the street nine years later. Taking inspiration from courtly love, this reignites the infatuation, which is both personal and transcendental. It is also tragic. Beatrice, already married to someone else, dies at the age of 24. She reappears, profoundly idealized, in his *Vita Nova* and *The Divine Comedy*.

Pair bonding and marriage in human societies is ubiquitous, yet scientists speculate that its roots may have little to do with love, possessiveness, passion, or even the division of labor. Research by Robin Dunbar suggests that the primary reason lies in the protection of otherwise vulnerable women, the "hired gun" theory, hence the widespread occurance of delicate beauties and their protective beasts.

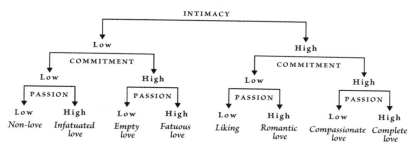

Above: Robert Sternberg's Triangular Theory of love. Psychologist Karen Horney identifies three styles of relating: moving toward, moving against, moving away. There's also moving together.

Above: A medieval "Fountain of Love" lets the love flow. From an edition of Boccaccio, 1499.

TRUST
fingers crossed

"Love all, trust a few, do wrong to none," says the Countess of Rousillon in Shakespeare's *All's Well That Ends Well*. But trusting someone with your heart, as shown opposite, is a risk so serious for an individual that many have great difficulty in taking it. As W.B. Yeats warned, "Tread softly because you tread on my dreams."

One of the most important aspects of any relationship is trust, an unwritten contract which bestows safety, reliability, and acceptance. Trust evolves over time, proven by words and deeds. Developmental psychologist Erik Erikson [1902-1994] identified trust as the first psychosocial stage of development, which is re-examined in successive stages throughout a lifetime. The English word for trust originates around the 12th century and is related to the Nordic *traust* (help), Old English *treowe* (faithful), Dutch *troost* (comfort), and German *trost* (consolation), as well as the English *true*.

In Homer's *Odyssey*, Odysseus, immediately after the birth of his son, leaves his beloved wife Penelope to fight in the Trojan War. Despite his absence for twenty years, Penelope remains faithful, rejecting over a hundred advances from other men (*see page 27*), using her beauty to beguile and bend them to her wishes. Odysseus likewise turns down promises of eternal youth, everlasting love, lust for battle, and all of the usual temptations offered a hero. They finally reunite, their mutual trust having carried them along the way.

Among the most essential elements of love are empathy, altruism, and compassion. Each represents a cycle of giving and receiving, sustaining through a transformative act of selflessness.

Above: Woman plucking a youth's heart from his chest, Florence, c. 1470.

Instead of giving your heart, why not try one of these:
Left: 19th-c. metal love token.
Right: Lover's guitar pick.

LOVE SICKNESS
there ain't no cure

People in love often find themselves so overcome with passion and desire that they show symptoms resembling sickness, addiction, or paranoid obsession, and many examples appear in classical literature.

In the 12th-century French legend *Tristan and Iseult*, Cornish king Mark sends his best knight (and nephew) Tristan to retrieve his future bride, Iseult, from Ireland. A love potion is prepared in the form of wine, and sent along for Iseult to drink, to make sure that she will love the older king. However, the brew is unwittingly drunk by Tristan and Iseult, who fall passionately in love. Brangwain, a handmaiden, discovers the deception, and tells the young couple they've just drunk their death. Tristan wonders whether this death is the pain of love, the punishment they will receive when discovered, or their eternal punishment in hell. Under love's spell, he says he will willingly accept them all. The potion points to the overwhelming power of love and attraction, which at the time challenged conventional marriage arrangements, often based upon politics and power. Here, instead, is a natural love between two individuals, with accompanying levels of emotional intensity, suffering, and tragedy.

The legend of *Lancelot and Guinevere* was also based upon the Tristan legend. King Arthur's most trusted knight and best friend Lancelot falls in love with his wife Queen Guinevere (and she with him). This most painful betrayal is discovered, leading to Guinevere's capture, although Lancelot rescues her from a death sentence. They live their remaining years apart, their love ultimately leading to the dissolution of the Knights of the Round Table.

Above: Midsummer drama. Lysander, under Puck's spell, pleads with Helena. A. Rackham, 1899.

Above: The giddy heights of love. Romeo and Juliet from an 1879 theater poster.

Above: Ophelia (from Hamlet) bewildered and heartbroken. E. Delacroix, 1843.

PERFECT
in the eye of the beholder

While beauty and aesthetics are largely a subjective affair, classical ideals have tended to favor balance and proportion.

Scientific studies in which babies were shown images of adult faces revealed that they gaze longest at those with the most symmetrical features. Symmetry and balance in the human form are usually identified as highly desirable genetic traits.

Other research has shown that males tend to favor females with large childlike eyes, and a waist-to-hip ratio at around 7:10, something more likely to appear on a young adult. Women, meanwhile, when looking for desirable men, prefer larger jawbones in economically depressed regions, but prefer softer features when resources are more plentiful.

In Ovid's story of the doomed *Echo and Narcissus*, Echo, cursed to repeat everything said to her, falls in love with Narcissus, who rejects her and becomes captivated instead by his own reflection.

Familiarity can also breed love. Elderly couples often come to love each other's every imperfect scar, wrinkle, and wart.

Opposite page: Attraction can sometimes be fatal. Tristan and Iseult on choppy waters (see page 38).

Above: A feast for the senses. Egyptian dancers and musicians, c. 1400 BC.

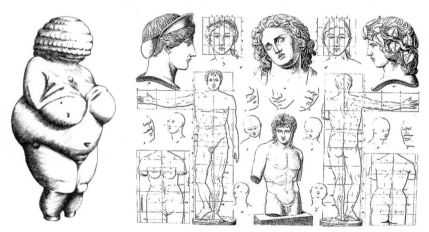

Above: The change in ideal form. Left: 23,000 year-old Venus of Willendorf figurine, drawing by Valentina Suma. Right: Classical Greek and Roman proportions.

SUN, MOON, AND STARS
thinking the world of someone

Metaphors of ideal love often include heavenly associations, and references to two lovers as pairs of celestial bodies appear in love stories across centuries and continents.

In Rustavelli's 12th-century Georgian tale *The Knight in Pantherskin*, there are two couples. In one, the hero, Advantil, is slender and in love with a princess, Tinatin (*see opposite*), who is likened to the Sun. The further he is from his beloved, the stronger her love shines on him, and the brighter he becomes, just like the moon. In the other couple the knight Tariel is solar and his princess, Nastan Darejan, is lunar.

Many Latin-based languages refer to the sun as male and the moon as female, while Germanic languages have them reversed. In Slavic languages, e.g. Russian, the Sun is neuter and the Moon female when full and male when a crescent. In Hebrew they take either gender.

In the Blackfoot Indian story *The Star Bride*, the mortal Feather Woman falls in love with Morning Star, son of the Sun and Moon. They give birth to Star Boy, who is brought back to Earth with a scar that only the Sun can remove. He falls in love with a woman, but she will not marry him with the scar, thus the purpose of the Sun Dance.

The astrological symbols representing Mars and Venus are used today as the symbols for male and female.

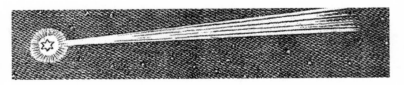

SURRENDER!
dying for love

Why do so many love stories entwine their theme with that of death? There are at least two purposes. The obvious one is to reveal the lover's dedication and willingness to forsake their personal welfare on behalf of their beloved, even to die. The other, according to thinkers like the mythologist Joseph Campbell [1904-1987], is metaphorical, where the sacrifice being made is of the ego. The necessary slaying of the dragon is the slaying of one's own shadow, insecurity, or separate ego which perceives the change presaged by love as a kind of death.

This level of devotion can be seen in Middle Eastern literature, wherein frequently the lovers do not consummate, but instead draw out their desire for unification into an ever-increasing rapture. The German philosopher Arthur Schopenhauer [1788-1860] explores this capacity to recognize that the other and the self are in fact one, using the word *Mitleid* (literally: suffering with; compassion).

The ancient Sanskrit phrase "Tat tvam asi" from the Vedic *Upanishads* reveals the same observation: "You are that, and that is you."

Above: St. George slays the dragon. Note the Queen and the human skull.

Above: A medieval love garden. Sweetness before surrender. Courtly courtship rituals, 1499.

Above: Cupid inflicting torments of love. Left: J. Caviceo, 1506. Right: L. Justiniano, 1506.

Opposite: Woman under the safeguard of knighthood, c.1490. Many knights had brothers in monastic orders, and the intertwining of the worldly and the divine is a feature of chivalric love.

ENGAGEMENT
and tying the knot

The traditional "on bended knee" marriage proposal is a custom in which surrender, honor, and respect are all expressed. The person being proposed to is exalted, as they have the power to determine the future of the relationship with the utterance of one simple word. In contrast, the proposer offers his or her whole self, without shame, from a position of (sometimes unaccustomed) vulnerability.

A circle represents eternity and the enclosing of a sacred space (the *temenos*). The wearing of a ring to symbolize betrothal started at least as early as ancient Rome. A man gave his beloved a ring of iron known as the *Annulus Pronubus* (noble ring) to announce not only his pledge to her, but her unavailability to others. The Greeks believed the fourth "ring" finger contained the longest vein in the body, extending straight to the heart, although the choice of finger and hand varies across history and culture. While marriages were largely civil contracts at that time, involving the exchange of family wealth and power, they later became religious affairs requiring officiation.

Worldwide, the most ancient forms of betrothal, e.g. handfasting, often include variations on the sacred tying of a knot.

Above: Three Forms of Marriage: For Worldly Love Officiated by Cupid; For Spiritual Love Officiated by Our Lord; For Wealth Officiated by the Devil. *J. Saenredam, after H. Goltzius, c. 1600.*

Above: Diamond solitaire, first introduced by Tiffany and Co. in the late 19th c. as a symbol of durability and brilliance; 7th c. gold Byzantine ring; 17th c. Irish Claddagh ring with heart (love), hands (friendship), and crown (loyalty).

Left: Tying the knot in style, Medici wedding, R. Gualtierotti , 1579.

Opposite left: A more modest country wedding. R. Cantagallina, c. 1620-40.

Opposite right: German ceremony, 1475.

MY OTHER HALF
joined at the hip

Once glued together, whether by custom or law, two people become one. Long periods of time together, as well as sharing life's ups and downs, deepen and strengthen bonds.

In Plato's *Symposium* [c. 380BC], Aristophanes, suggesting why lovers feel whole when together, speculates that humans were once united with two heads, four hands and four feet, and came in three sexes: male, female, and androgynous/hermaphroditic. However, they were an arrogant species and Zeus (as usual) lost his patience and split their bodies in half. Ever since they have been running around seeking their other halves. Symbols of the unity of opposites such as the Chinese Yin-Yang are present across many traditions and cultures.

Jung described the ideal pairing of female and male, or their inner counterparts *anima* and *animus*, as a *syzygy*. This condition allows for the complete individuation and realization of each member of the pair. As with a perfectly balanced contrapuntal music composition, independence and interdependence exist in equal measure.

Above: Alchemical Symbolism, from
The Rosary of the Philosophers, 1550.

Above: Christian creation, a Hungarian
Adam and Eve. Artist unknown.

Left: Reunion of Soul and Body, after Blake, 1813. Right: Elephants, like many animals, mate
for life. Opposite: Alchemical unions, one of the most widely shared mysteries of them all.

LOVEMAKING
everybody needs somebody

The innate urge to procreate underpins all the chemistry and biology necessary for the act itself to take place. As the heroine of a 2002 movie says, "It's called sex! It's fun! You should try it!"

The ancient Hindu *Kama Sutra* [c. 300 BC] lists various types of sexual arts, including kissing, marking with teeth and nails, embracing, touching, rubbing, piercing, pressing, striking, moaning, and coitus. Of the latter there are 40 basic positions, with variations limited only by imagination and age, some with poetic names like "the ripe mango plum," "climbing the tree," and "the caress of the bud." For those who still have the energy, it also advises the study of singing, music, and dance. The later 11th-century *Ratirahasya,* or *Koka Shastra* (*Secrets of Love*) is likewise full of practical guidance and adds a study of feminine beauty, erogenous zones, aphrodisiacs, and ideal days for arousal, but instructs that these sacred arts are only to be enjoyed within marriage.

Ancient taboos around incest or premarital sex are common the world over. In the case of the latter, before the invention of contraception, the costs were different for each partner as a young mother is tied to her child in a way in which the father is not. This often observed difference between the sexes is neatly summed up in a line from the 1991 film *City Slickers*: "Women need a reason to have sex. Men just need a place."

i.

This page: Three medieval images showing sex symbolism, Netherlands, 1470. i) A man asks a lady if he can put a ferret into a hole. ii) A gentleman asks a maiden if he may unlock her casket. iii) A knight shows his intentions to storm his lady's castle via a particular portal.

Opposite: Simple clues to sex positions. 13th-century theologian Albertus Magnus, (not a fan of the Kama Sutra) listed five sexual positions in order of most to least appropriate: 1) missionary, 2) side-to-side, 3) sitting, 4) standing, and 5) "a tergo" (from behind). He deemed missionary as the only natural position; the others were "morally questionable."

ii.

iii.

THE FRUITS OF LOVE
the renewal of the home

Perhaps the greatest gifts from happy unions can be children. These little darlings give parents the opportunity to see the world through new eyes, and learn more about themselves and about the joys and struggles their own parents faced. Love and devotion combine into a potent mix of daily selfless sacrifice.

Devotion to service, land, or art can be just as profound. Dedication to a place or task is just as much an act of love. A teacher helps their students develop, a gardener takes delight in their garden *(see opposite below right)*, a captain loves their ship and crew, a musician is married to their music, an artist to their art and so on. Love in all cases is the glue, the cause and the effect of the bond. The prison of the separate ego is transcended and introspection gives way to outrospection.

In romantic love, a couple's early phase of intense excitement mellows into a sweeter conscious committment to nurture each other and grow together. Over time, this mature love emanates towards those around them. Their house becomes the loving home that we all know and recognize; we met it earlier in the book.

Above: Medieval Christian view of conception.

Left: Children. G. Raverat, 1926.

Right: A life can be devoted to growing. From The Gardener's Labyrinth *by Thomas Hill, England, 1577.*

Opposite page: Harvest under a crescent moon. *S. Palmer, c. 1826.*

LOVE IS ALL AROUND
what a wonderful world

The call to love is to love not only others, but also ourselves and all things. Not an easy task, so many give up. The tragedy of love is not in the separation of lovers, but in the separation of people from love.

If we were more aware of the love we receive, then, like the Three Graces (*see page 24*), we might give more back to the world around us. Over a lifetime, we can move from being egocentric, to ethnocentric, to world-centric, gradually increasing our capacity for love.

Ancient cultures and belief systems describe numerous ways of perceiving, sensing, and expressing this most potent of energies. In outline, *instincts* are the foundation, *emotions* are the inflections, and *thoughts* are the interpretations of our inexorable propensity to love.

Modern science also tells us that love is given and received through three the centers of *mind* (cerebral cortex), *heart* (limbic system, *page 10*) and *body* (autonomic nervous system).

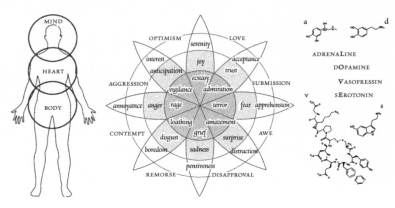

Above: The Planet Venus and Her Children, *Florence, 1464-5.*

Opposite center: Plutchik's Wheel. *The primary emotions are Joy, Trust, Fear, Surprise, Sadness, Anticipation, Anger, and Disgust; each has an opposite, e.g. Sadness/Joy. The intensity of related emotions increases and decreases as you move towards or away from the center. Love is a dyad requiring degrees of joy and trust for it to exist.*

ONE LOVE
the song of the universe

Across the world, ancient traditions speak of there being a unity in multiplicity, that the All is, in some veiled way, also the One. For people who study these traditions, the same is true of love – perhaps there is just one source, one spring which nourishes us all.

In Jami's 12th-century Persian love story *Yusuf and Zulaikha*, handsome Yusuf becomes the object of Zulaika's desire, but does not respond to her advances (he is purely interested in the divine). Zulaikha tries everything, even building an erotic palace of mirrors to enchant her beloved, but Yusuf is unmoved. Eventually she realizes that Earthly love is merely the shadow of a higher love, and will always disappoint. She becomes wise, and finally, one day, many years later, Yusuf hears her singing, and their eyes lock in a deep, shared love.

The opposite of separation is unification. As Bob Marley put it, "Love the life you live; live the life you love." In the same way, the Golden Rule advises: "Treat others as you would be treated yourself," once again collapsing self and other into one. Becoming a loving member of the shared whole is to love all things.

Love really might make the world go round. The new era of quantum mechanics has revealed how everything at a fundamental level is truly connected, as our ancestors once knew. Add love into the mix, and it follows that the entire universe may be suffused with this life-giving force. Thus love propagates itself, radiates across time and space, and like any timeless melody, sings to us all.

The Sparkling Circles of the Heavenly Host, *from Dante's* Divine Comedy
(see pages 32-34). Etching by G. Dore, 1868.

APPENDIX

"I love you" in 67 languages

AFRIKAANS - Ek het jou lief
ALBANIAN - Te dua
ARABIC - Ana behibak (to male)
ARABIC - Ana behibek (to female)
ARMENIAN - Yes kez sirumem
BENGALI - Ami tomake bhalobashi
BELARUSIAN - Ya tabe kahayu
BULGARIAN - Obicham te
CAMBODIAN - Soro lahn nhee ah
CATALAN - T'estimo
CANTONESE - Ngo oiy ney a
MANDARIN - Wo ai ni (pr. "War I knee")
CREOLE - Mi aime jou
CROATIAN - Volim te
CZECH - Miluji te. **SLOVAK** - Lu'bim ta
DANISH - Jeg elsker dig
DUTCH - Ik hou van jou
ENGLISH - I love you
ESTONIAN - Ma armastan sind
ETHIOPIAN - Afgreki'
FARSI - Doset daram
FILIPINO - Mahal kita
FINNISH - Mina rakastan sinua
FRENCH - Je t'aime, Je t'adore
GAELIC - Ta gra agam ort
GEORGIAN - Mikvarhar
GERMAN - Ich liebe dich
GREEK - S'agapo
GUJARATI - Hoo thunay prem karoo choo
HAWAIIAN - Aloha Au ia' oe
HEBREW - Ani ohev otach (male to female)
HEBREW - Ohevet ot'cha (female to male)
HINDI - Hum tumhe pyar karte hae
HUNGARIAN - Szeretlek

ICELANDIC - Eg elska tig
INDONESIAN - Saya cinta padamu
IRISH - Taim i' ngra leat
ITALIAN - Ti amo
JAPANESE - Aishiteru
KOALA - Bajaba
KOREAN - Sarang Heyo
LATIN - Te amo
LATVIAN - Es tevi miilu
LEBANESE - Bahibak
LITHUANIAN - Tave myliu
MACEDONIAN - Te sakam
MALAY - Saya cintakan mu padamu
MALTESE - Inhobbok
MOROCCAN - Ana moajaba bik
NORWEGIAN - Jeg elsker deg
POLISH - Kocham ciebie
PORTUGUESE - Eu te amo
ROMANIAN - Te iubesc
RUSSIAN - Ya tebya liubliu
SERBIAN - Volim te
SLOVENIAN - Ljubim te
SPANISH - Te quiero / Te amo
SWEDISH - Jag alskar dig
TAIWANESE - Wa ga ei li
TAHITIAN - Ua here vau ia oe
THAI - Phom rak khun
TUNISIAN - Ha eh bak
TURKISH - Seni seviyorum
UKRAINIAN - Ya tebe kahayu
URDU - mai aap say pyaar karta hoo
VIETNAMESE - Anh ye u em
WELSH - Rwy n dy garu di
YIDDISH - Ikh hob dikh